AN AWFULLY BEASTLY BUSINESS

SAVING A SEA MONSTER

(An adaptation taken from Sea
Monsters and Other Delicacies)

Written by The Beastly Boys
Adapted by Maureen Haselhurst
Illustrated by Jonny Duddle

6

Published by Pearson Education Limited, Edinburgh Gate, Harlow, Essex, CM20 2JE
Registered company number: 872828

www.pearsonschools.co.uk

Adapted text based on *Sea Monsters and Other Delicacies*, originally published by Simon &
Schuster Children's Books in 2008.
Copyright © Matthew Morgan, David Sinden and Guy Macdonald 2008
Interior illustrations copyright © Jonny Duddle 2008
Cover illustration copyright © Jonny Duddle 2010

Adaptation by Maureen Haselhurst

Cover/interior illustrations and text all used by kind permission of Simon & Schuster
Children's Books.

The rights of Matthew Morgan, David Sinden and Guy Macdonald to be identified
as authors of this work have been asserted by them in accordance with the Copyright,
Designs and Patents Act 1988.

First published 2011

15 14 13 12
10 9 8 7 6 5 4 3 2

British Library Cataloguing in Publication Data
A catalogue record for this book is available from the British Library

ISBN 978 1 408 27394 4

Copyright notice

Printed and bound in Malaysia, CTP–VP

Acknowledgements
We would like to thank the children and teachers of Bangor Central Integrated
Primary School, NI; Bishop Henderson C of E Primary School, Somerset;
Brookside Community Primary School, Somerset; Cheddington Combined School,
Buckinghamshire; Cofton Primary School, Birmingham; Dair House Independent
School, Buckinghamshire; Deal Parochial School, Kent; Newbold Riverside Primary
School, Rugby and Windmill Primary School, Oxford for their invaluable help in the
development and trialling of the Bug Club resources.

Every effort has been made to contact copyright holders of material reproduced in this
book. Any omissions will be rectified in subsequent printings if notice is given to the
publishers.

Visit the Beastly Business website for lots of exciting extras – meet the authors,
join the RSPCB and discover the secrets of the beasts…!

CONTENTS

ROYAL SOCIETY FOR THE PREVENTION OF CRUELTY TO BEASTS

·RSPCB·

"I DO SOLEMNLY
SWEAR TO PRESERVE
AND PROTECT THE
WILD. FROM THIS DAY
FORTH I PLEDGE MY
ALLEGIANCE
TO BEASTS."

CHAPTER ONE

Something truly awesome was wallowing in the deep water of an underground tank. A boy and a young woman were watching it through a huge window in the wall.

"Wow! It's gigantic. What is it, Dr Fielding?" the boy asked.

"It's an extremely rare sea monster, Ulf," Dr Fielding told him. "A Redback, most of which have been hunted to extinction. This one's an adult female. I would guess that she's around 150 years old."

Ulf stared at the gigantic beast. It resembled an enormous, armoured octopus with eight tentacles as thick and long as tree trunks. Its head was covered by a hard, spiky shell of red coral, studded with ancient barnacles. Bulbous green eyes bulged out of its craggy face and fixed themselves on Ulf.

"Is there any chance I can swim with her?" he asked eagerly.

Dr Fielding shook her head. "Forget it, Ulf. Nobody ever swims with Redbacks."

"I've swum with elephant eels and bazooka rays and skewerhead serpents and megamaul crabs, so what's different about this one?" Ulf protested.

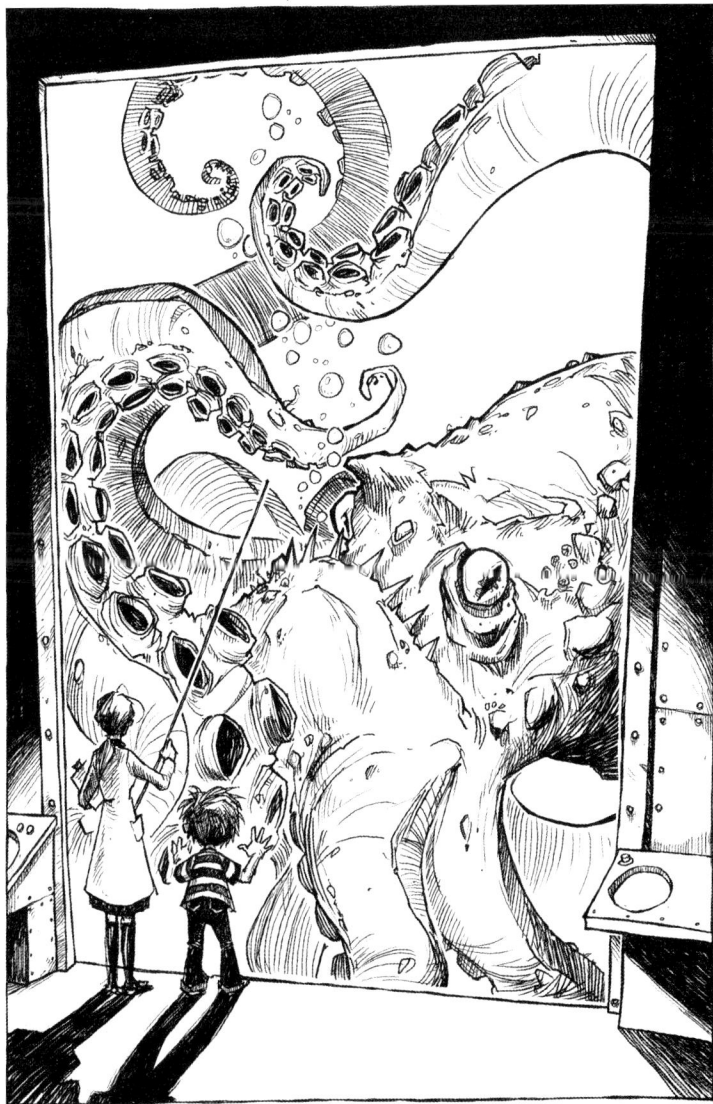

"It's deadly," she told him. "The Redback is probably the most venomous creature on the planet."

Ulf stared at the sea beast respectfully. It certainly was impressive.

"Why's she in the examination tank?" he asked. "What's wrong with her?"

"I'm not sure, exactly," replied Dr Fielding. "She was found tangled up in a fishing net. Three of her tentacles seem to be paralysed. It would appear that something – or someone – has attacked her. She's in a bad way, I'm afraid."

Ulf looked up at Dr Fielding. "Another job for the RSPCB!"

★   ★   ★

The Royal Society for the Prevention of Cruelty to Beasts was a rescue centre for rare and endangered beasts. Its headquarters were a remote old house called Farraway Hall set in a huge beast park and it had been Ulf's home for over ten years. Dr Fielding was the RSPCB's vet. No beast was too huge, too ugly or too dangerous for her to care for

"Have a look at this," Dr Fielding said, handing Ulf an X-ray. "You might find it interesting."

Ulf held it up to the light and shuddered. The sea monster's insides were not a pretty sight. Its stomach was cave-like and filled with half-eaten sharks.

Suddenly, the beast let out a loud, rumbling bellow that shook the window of the viewing gallery.

"She's in a lot of pain," muttered Dr Fielding. "I'm not surprised. Look at that."

The X-ray showed a jagged fracture line running around the top of the shell. Beneath it was something white and as big as a barrel.

"That's some brain!" gasped Ulf in amazement.

"Yes, but look at the dark shadow in the centre. It appears there's a blood clot – a ball of thick, hard blood – and they're bad news."

Ulf stared at it. "But you can operate, can't you?"

Dr Fielding put her hand on his shoulder. "Operating on a Redback is too dangerous, Ulf. I'll show you why."

She rapped on the viewing window.

As quickly as lightning, the monster lashed out at her, pounding the window with its five working tentacles. At the same time, the rocky slabs of its coral shell began to move apart and a snake-like limb slithered out from a hole between the creature's eyes.

"That's the Redback's stinger," Dr Fielding explained. "It injects the heart of its prey with immobilising venom. Then it eats the prey alive."

"Okay, she's a bit creepy, but it's no reason to let her die," pleaded Ulf.

"It's just too dangerous," said Dr Fielding firmly. "I'm sorry, but we can't save every beast."

"I'm a beast," he muttered, "and you saved me."

Dr Fielding smiled at him. Ulf was right. He too was one of the beasts who had been rescued by the RSPCB. Ten years previously he had been found as a tiny, abandoned werecub. Now he was an eleven-year-old boy werewolf and every month on the night of the full moon he would transform from boy to wolf.

"You're only dangerous once a month. For the rest of the time you're just a cheeky kid!"

"But Dr Fielding—"

"Be sensible, Ulf," Dr Fielding said seriously. "It's impossible to operate without getting rid of the venom."

Ulf's eyes lit up. "I know! What about using that old venom extractor back at the house?"

"If you mean that old contraption in the Room of Curiosities, it would never work," she told him.

"How do we know that it won't work unless we try?" demanded Ulf, and he sprinted away.

"No! It's far too dangerous!" shouted Dr Fielding.

She was too late. Ulf had already leaped onto his quad bike and was accelerating off towards Farraway Hall.

ROYAL SOCIETY FOR THE PREVENTION OF CRUELTY TO BEASTS · RSPCB ·

CHAPTER TWO

Ulf parked his quad bike at the front door of Farraway Hall and hurtled up the shadowy staircase to a room high on the upper floors where all the old RSPCB artefacts were stored. It was known as the Room of Curiosities, and it was full of secrets.

He opened the door and ducked as a colony of sabre-toothed bats flapped and swirled around his head.

He weaved between the curtains of filthy cobwebs to the display cabinets and peered through the dusty glass. There, amongst a rusting pile of antique vets' tools, was a strange-looking object. It was made from an old-fashioned leather football with a handle on either side. Attached to the base of the ball was an old tin flask. Unfortunately, a clawhammer beetle, the size of a rat, was snoozing on top of it.

Ulf prised the cabinet door open. The clawhammer scuttled into the corner and clicked its pincers threateningly.

Ignoring it, Ulf pulled out the curious contraption.

Printed on the old leather were two words:

VENOM EXTRACTOR

"Got it!" shouted Ulf triumphantly.

On the other side of the ball were some instructions.

User Instructions

1. When approaching Redback, the user must hold extractor in front of his/her heart.
2. When stinger strikes, fangs will penetrate ball and inject venom.
3. Venom sacks are empty when tip of stinger changes from blue to black.
4. Redback is now safe to handle.

DEADLY IMPORTANT!

As stinger is guided by the user's heartbeat, it is essential that the extractor is placed in front of the chest to protect his/her heart.

Ulf sprinted out of the house, kick-started the quad bike and, twisting back the throttle, he sped off towards the lagoon.

Reaching the dockside, he pulled up with a screech and ran over to the examination tank. He stared into the deep water and there the sea monster was, coiled and menacing.

There was no time to think about what he was doing. Gripping the handles of the venom extractor, Ulf took a deep breath and jumped.

★   ★   ★

He hit the cold water and his body gave a shudder. His chest tightened, and his wet T-shirt and jeans clung to his skin.

Seeing him in the water, the Redback began to writhe around furiously, banging its shell against the underwater gate to the lagoon as a warning. Five of its tentacles were thrashing wildly, coiling up the walls. The other three hung limply, dragging along the concrete floor.

Clutching the venom extractor's handles, Ulf dived down.

The huge beast's green eyes bulged as it saw Ulf. It let out a low, menacing bellow and its tentacles whipped down from the walls and ploughed through the water towards him.

Ulf steadied himself, cold with dread,

as the Redback loomed large, trying to pull itself towards him. Its body was tilted to one side and its tentacles jerked. It was obviously injured, but still capable of killing him.

Suddenly, one of the tentacles whipped forwards through the water. Ulf dived beneath it and the tentacle thudded against the side of the examination bay.

Another tentacle swept up and Ulf felt its barnacles scrape against his leg, knocking him sideways.

The sound of rapping echoed through the water. Ulf turned to see Dr Fielding banging on the viewing window, screaming something that he couldn't hear.

He turned back just in time to see another tentacle slamming towards him. It whacked him in the stomach, sending him somersaulting backwards through the water.

He regained his balance and dodged as another tentacle swept over his head. The Redback was moving in on him.

★　　★　　★

Ulf gripped the venom extractor tightly.

There was a low scraping sound and a rumble of rocks as the sea monster's mouth opened like a cave. Ulf could see the half-eaten sharks floating inside. If he weren't careful, he would be joining them.

His heart thumped in his chest as he watched the stinger emerging from a hole just above the sea monster's eyes. The snake-like limb slid out through the beast's coral shell, pulsing with ice-blue venom. It weaved towards him, sensing his heartbeat.

Ulf trembled as the stinger flicked out its tongue. At that moment, a tentacle swung round and struck him on the back, knocking the venom extractor from his hands. Up, up, up it rose through the water, floating away from his grasp! The tentacle slid around him and gripped him by the waist, its suckers oozing black oil.

Desperate, Ulf kicked and struggled, clawing at the tentacle, trying to prise it off.

He glanced at the stinger. It was uncoiling slowly but surely; the vibrations of his heartbeat guiding it towards its target.

I'm going to die, he thought.

★   ★   ★

For a split second the tentacle lost its grip. Ulf grasped the opportunity. He wriggled and squirmed violently until he slid out of the sea monster's hold.

Then mustering all his strength, Ulf shot upwards. The blue tip of the stinger was opening and its snake-like fangs were raised, ready to strike. The venom extractor was just within his grasp. Ulf lunged forward and desperately made a grab for it.

"Got it!" and he pressed it close to his chest.

He felt an almighty thump as the stinger struck at his heart. The venom extractor shook wildly as the sharp fangs pierced the ball. The stinger writhed, but its fangs were firmly locked in the leather. Ulf gripped the handles tightly, struggling to keep hold of the ball. His heart was hammering in his chest, his knuckles were white and his arms ached. He could feel the extractor getting colder as the icy venom trickled down into the flask. The stinger's pulsating tip was gradually changing colour from blue to black.

Suddenly, the stinger released the ball. It swayed in front of Ulf, flicking out its tongue. It snaked up and down Ulf's body, probing him inquisitively. It seemed curious that he was still moving.

Now that its venom sacks were empty, the Redback sensed that it had lost its prey and its stinger snaked back into the hole in its coral shell.

Ulf kicked hard and broke the surface, gasping for air. He grabbed the side of the tank and heaved himself out.

Dr Fielding ran up to him and threw her arms around him, hugging him, rubbing him to warm him up.

"W-well, I s--said I w--wanted to sw-sw-swim with the Redback," he joked feebly.

"It's not funny, Ulf!" she scolded. "Never do that again. It was utterly reckless!"

"B-b-ut, the v-v-venom ex-ex-extractor w-works," Ulf jabbered, his teeth chattering with cold.

Dr Fielding took the curious device from him and examined it.

"How extraordinary," she murmured and patted Ulf's arm. "It's safe to operate on her now, thanks to you," she smiled. "Although I'm not sure how we're going to manage her – she's a big girl."

Ulf grinned. "I think this is a job for Orson," he said.

ROYAL SOCIETY FOR THE PREVENTION OF CRUELTY TO BEASTS · RSPCB ·

CHAPTER THREE

Orson was a particularly hulky giant. He was a friend of Ulf's and another of the RSPCB's success stories. He helped out with the heavier jobs at the rescue centre.

Dr Fielding looked up as he clumped along the dockside towards them. "Just the beast we've been looking for," she smiled. "Is there any chance you can raise my latest patient to the surface?"

Orson peered into the examination

tank. "Well, well, what a little beauty," he said. "No problem, Dr Fielding."

Together, Orson and Ulf went off to the marine store to collect the equipment that was needed.

Soon, they had lined up eight yellow flotation barrels and a pile of bungee ropes along the edge of the examination bay. The giant lowered himself into the water and swam across the tank, floating a barrel in front of him. The sea monster was floundering on the bottom of the tank, watching him suspiciously. One of its tentacles reached up and wrapped around his massive shoulders.

"Easy, girl," Orson said, gently peeling the tentacle off with his shovel-sized hand.

"Catch!" Ulf called as he threw

Orson one of the bungee ropes.

Orson pushed the yellow barrel under the water, took a deep breath and dived down. Taking hold of a tentacle, he tied the barrel to it with the bungee rope. A moment later the barrel bobbed to the surface, lifting the tentacle with it.

Orson came up for air as another tentacle reached for him. He caught it, pulling the sea monster towards him, and attached the second barrel. The remaining tentacles churned the water as he pushed the third barrel down.

One by one, Orson attached all eight barrels. Slowly, the sea monster began to float upwards until, at last, its red shell broke through the surface.

Ulf watched it, mesmerised. The Redback was so huge that its shell could have been a coral island. He jumped back as five of the tentacles coiled their way up the walls of the tank while the other three lay limp on the surface of the water.

Dr Fielding came out of the marine store carrying her medical bag, a circular saw and a suction pump. "Can you bring that bucket, please, Ulf?" she asked.

Ulf peered inside. It was full of wet cement. Whatever was she going to do with cement? But there was no time to ask questions – they had an operation to do.

"Could you tether the sea monster securely, please, Orson?" she called.

The giant swam around the examination bay, firmly tying each tentacle to the steel harnessing rings that were bolted to the walls.

"Don't worry, girl," Orson whispered to the beast. "Dr Fielding will fix you up." He stroked one of its tentacles, checking the rope was secure. Then he slid a wooden plank from the edge of the examination bay to the top of the sea monster's shell.

That was it. Everything was ready.

★   ★   ★

Dr Fielding carried her medical bag and tools along the plank and stepped nimbly onto the sea monster. She climbed down the front of its shell to a ledge about a metre above its eyes.

"Come on, Ulf. It's perfectly safe," she called.

Ulf heaved the bucket along the

plank. He stepped off onto the sea monster's coral shell, his bare feet scraping against the barnacles. He passed the bucket down, then stepped onto the ledge.

Dr Fielding was laying out her tools. "You might see a lot of blood," she said.

"I'll be okay," Ulf told her, trying to sound confident. He didn't mind blood when he was a wolf, but wasn't so keen when he was a boy.

Dr Fielding started examining the sea monster's shell and ran her fingers over a jagged crack that was at least a metre long. "This is the fracture, Ulf. Its brain is directly underneath it."

Dr Fielding picked up the circular saw. "Right then," she said. "Let's take a look at it."

Ulf stared at the tool nervously. At the front of it was a large, circular blade with jagged metal teeth. "Won't that hurt her?" he asked.

Dr Fielding flicked a switch and the metal blade started to spin. "No. It has no feeling in its shell," she shouted over the sound of the screeching blade.

Ulf watched as Dr Fielding pressed the saw into the sea monster's shell. Bright sparks flew as the blade whirred and screamed through the hard coral. She cut a wide circle around the fracture until a large slab of shell was loosened. Then she switched the saw off and pulled at the loose slab.

"I'm going to need help with this, Ulf," she panted.

Ulf and Dr Fielding heaved at the coral. There was a repulsive sucking sound and it lifted off like a lid. Ulf peered nervously into the large hole it had left. The Redback's brain was a vast mass of spongy white flesh criss-crossed with veins.

"That's impressive," he gasped. "But why is it sitting in a pool of blood?"

CHAPTER FOUR

Dr Fielding passed Ulf a metal canister fitted with a rubber hose. "This is a suction pump," she told him. "I need the brain totally drained, so please make sure you suck all of that blood out."

Ulf poked the hose into the pool of blood around the monstrous brain. The suction pump gurgled as blood began to bubble up the hose and into the canister. The sound made him feel sick.

Oh, please don't let me be sick, he thought. It would be so embarrassing.

There was no time to think about himself. Dr Fielding had put her head torch on and was already peering into the hole. "We need to find the source of the bleeding," she said, as the torchlight illuminated the bulging brain.

"It's big," Ulf said.

"It needs to be. A sea monster's brain is highly specialised," Dr Fielding told him. "The Redback's brain is divided into different parts – or lobes, as we call them," she explained. "Each lobe is responsible for a different function."

She pointed to two large bulges covered with a slimy membrane. "Those lobes control all the functions that the creature needs to live in deep water. Both of them look fine."

One by one she examined the different lobes and found nothing wrong. Ulf moved the suction hose closer. He was so fascinated by what he was seeing that he'd forgotten all about feeling sick.

"Now, Ulf, have a look at this," Dr Fielding said. "This is how the Redback senses vibrations in the water."

She reached deep down the front of the brain to where a small black bulge was nestled in a thick bundle of nerves. She shone her torch into a cavity that ran down inside the shell.

Ulf leaned in and looked down. The nerves were twisted together into a snake-like tube, covered in scales.

"That's its stinger!" he said in amazement.

"Yes, and it's harmless now, thanks to you," smiled Dr Fielding. "It'll take a day or two to replenish its venom, so we're safe for the moment." She got back to business and reached into the back of the brain.

"This over here is the lobe that controls the Redback's movement," she told him.

She carefully slid her hands down either side of the bulge and her eyes widened. "Oh my goodness," she gasped.

"What's the matter?" Ulf asked.

"I've found the problem, Ulf."

Dr Fielding gently pushed her hand further in, parting the spongy flesh. Bulging up from the white brain tissue was a huge red lump.

"Whatever's that?" Ulf asked.

"It's the blood clot we saw on the X-ray," she explained. "One of the main arteries that takes blood to the brain has burst. This part of the brain isn't working properly. That's why some of the tentacles are paralysed."

"Can you fix it?"

"It'll be tricky. We'll have to perform an arterial bypass."

Ulf looked confused. "How do we do that?" he asked.

"We have to get rid of the blood clot. So, first of all, we'll have to replace the damaged artery with a synthetic one – one that's man-made."

"Then what?" asked Ulf.

"Then we remove the clot. However, it's important that we seal off the blood supply while we're operating."

She looked at Ulf gravely. "This is a risky operation. If it goes wrong, then the tentacles will be permanently paralysed. If that happens, she'll die."

★   ★   ★

"Now, when I say so, I need you to hold that blood clot for me," Dr Fielding said.

She took out a laser pen, two metal clips and a length of thin rubber tubing.

"This is the synthetic blood vessel. We'll use it to replace the burst artery."

She looked across to Orson, who was pacing along the side of the examination bay, looking extremely worried.

"Can you make sure that she stays still, please, Orson? We're at a tricky part of the operation."

"No problem," the giant called back. He slipped into the water and began to tighten the ropes that held the tentacles. "She's secure."

Dr Fielding parted the upper lobes of the brain. Ulf could see the huge red clot. "Lift it up," she told him.

Ulf cupped his hands around the blood clot. It felt sticky and warm. As he lifted it, he saw a thick blood vessel running under it.

"That's the ruptured artery that needs to be replaced," Dr Fielding said. She carefully clipped the metal clips to it, either side of the clot. "That's it.

The blood flow is sealed off. We'll have to work quickly."

Ulf glanced up. All the sea monster's tentacles had gone limp.

"Concentrate, Ulf."

He held the clot steady as Dr Fielding took her laser pen and pressed its tip to the artery. Ulf saw a glowing red dot as the laser burned a small hole in the artery wall. She then repeated the procedure, burning a second hole in the artery on the other side of the clot.

She switched the laser pen off and, with a micro-needle and thread, stitched the ends of the synthetic blood vessel onto the edges of the two holes. Taking a pair of small scissors, she deftly snipped the clot from the damaged artery. Ulf felt it come free in his hands. It was heavy and wobbled like a raspberry jelly as he lifted it out.

"Perfect," Dr Fielding said.

She held a specimen bag open and Ulf dropped the clot inside it. "Now let's see if the bypass has worked."

She unfastened the metal clips and blood began to flow through the synthetic artery.

"You've mended it!" Ulf cheered.

"Don't get your hopes up yet. We won't know definitely for a minute or two."

★ ★ ★

The minutes passed. The Redback's tentacles were still hanging limply from their bungee ropes. Ulf's hopes began to fade.

"Tell me if you see any sign of movement, Orson," Dr Fielding called over to him.

Orson gave a thumbs-up. "Will do," he replied.

"Right then, Ulf. Let's get the shell back on," she said.

Together, they reached across and replaced the huge slab of shell back into the hole.

"Can you manage to seal it up?" asked Dr Fielding, handing Ulf a trowel. So that was what the wet cement was for!

Carefully, Ulf began to spread the cement into the circular cut in the shell and then along the jagged crack. When he had finished, the shell was as good as new.

"Excellent job," nodded Dr Fielding

and then she turned to Orson. "You can start releasing the tentacles now."

The giant swam effortlessly around the examination bay, untying the tentacles from the metal rings. Ulf watched with dismay as they fell limply into the water.

"We've done all we can," Dr Fielding murmured, trying to hide the anxiety in her voice.

Now all they could do was watch and wait. Minutes passed and the Redback's monstrous tentacles still hung limply in the water.

★   ★   ★

Orson put his great arm around Ulf's shoulder. "Don't worry, you've done your best," he said. But then he stopped and pointed to the far corner of the examination bay. "Hang on. Look at that!" he whispered.

The tip of one of the tentacles was twitching. Then another began to stir.

"It's working!" Ulf gasped.

One by one, all of the tentacles slowly came to life, calmly swaying back and forth in the water. They began exploring the examination bay, feeling the walls and touching the flotation barrels. The tip of one tentacle reached up and felt the mended section of shell where the operation had been performed.

Ulf crossed his fingers and asked, "Will she be all right now?"

Dr Fielding beamed in relief. "She's going to be fine, Ulf, thanks to you."

ROYAL SOCIETY FOR THE PREVENTION OF CRUELTY TO BEASTS

·RSPCB·

CHAPTER FIVE

That night, the stillness was broken by the sound of grating metal. Ulf and Dr Fielding stood on the dockside as Orson opened the automatic sea gates to the lagoon. It was time to set the Redback free.

"It's a pity she can't stay with us," Ulf said sadly. "She might have learned to let me swim with her."

"She wouldn't," replied Dr Fielding. "She's a wild, wild beast, Ulf. She would never let a human swim with her."

Orson pointed into the lagoon. "Look, she's on the move."

The Redback sensed the open water. With a powerful thrust of her tentacles, she shot out of the lagoon like a torpedo. They watched the churning waves that marked her passage until she was lost in the dark ocean.

Dr Fielding yawned. "It's well past my bedtime," she smiled. "Good night," and she set off for Farraway Hall.

Orson looked at the horizon and nudged Ulf. "Moon's coming up," he said and strode away.

★   ★   ★

Ulf stared up at the night sky. The full moon was on the rise.

He felt a familiar itching and saw that the hair on the back of his hands was spreading. His nails were extending and turning claw-like. His body shuddered as his skeleton shifted. Thick hair sprouted from his head to the tip of his tail. Fangs split through his gums and his tongue started dripping with saliva. His lower jaw thrust forwards as his face twisted into that of a wolf. Ulf the werewolf lifted his head towards the moon and howled.

A thunderous roar vibrated from deep below the ocean. A tentacle, thick as a tree trunk, rose above the water and swirled through the air as if it were beckoning.

Ulf padded towards the sea, swishing his wolf tail. She'll never swim with a human, he thought, but perhaps she'll swim with a beast.

He gazed out at the dark ocean and walked into the waves ...

THE END ... FOR NOW!